PREFACE

The Alpha Course which was started at Holy T (HTB) has caught the imagination of large nun evangelism in today's climate. However it has concern among many. What might there be in it ⸺ ⸺⸺ it, that causes these doubts and hesitations? This booklet seeks to help you clarify possible apprehensions and questions.

The booklet contains a critique of the Alpha course, based on its videos and other HTB material, which Elizabeth McDonald orginally put together for her home church. It is a personal assessment, and not exhaustive, but we believe it will be valuable to you in making your own appraisal because it has already proved so for others. The booklet also contains an article on the Alpha course reprinted with permission from 'Evangelicals Now' of December 1995 in Appendix 1.

Elizabeth McDonald also added in a letter to me that, in her opinion, Nicky Gumbel over-emphasises what we are saved *to* at the expense of what we are saved *from*. This imbalance is a general trend in 'new' evangelical circles at present and seems to be increasing in prominence particularly in those churches which have embraced the Toronto Blessing [the two often go together]. It stems from teaching that God is primarily love when the scriptures point to the primary characteristic of God as being holy. God's holiness is mentioned twice as many times in scripture than his nature as love or loving. In fact no gospel message in Acts proclaims God's love for sinners – see Appendix 2. The result of emphasising God's love is that the need of repentance for sin and the consequences of that sin in the sight of a holy God who must and will judge it is hardly mentioned. Christians are being presented with a deficient, deceptive and dangerous understanding of God and the basis of our relationship with Him. I am convinced that there are now many in the churches who believe they are Christians but are not, because they have never truly repented of sin, and become dependent on Jesus Christ both as Saviour and Lord. The result is a church which is in many respects no different to the world and is also wide open to receive every deceptive teaching and activity presented to it. The Bleeding of the Evangelical Church by David Wells, [Banner of Truth Publications ISBN 0-85151-682-3] is a useful booklet dealing with this issue, and is available priced £1 from booksellers.

However, regarding an assessment of the Alpha course in a particular church, you need to bear in mind that if a church is concerned to present the biblical gospel, that they may be using the practical organisation of Alpha but have substituted a bible based course they have written themselves instead of the recommended course videos and books etc.

Jo Gardner, Adullam Register May 1996

First published in Great Britain in 1996
by
St Matthew Publications
Copyright © Elizabeth McDonald

ISBN 0 9524672 6 7

Further copies of this book are available in some bookshops or can be ordered from:
St Matthew Publications, 24 Geldart St, Cambridge CB1 2LX UK
Tel: +44 (0)1223 363545, Fax +44 (0)1223 512304
Email: aak66@dial.pipex.com
http:www.phar.cam.ac.uk/StMatts/

ALPHA:
New Life or New Lifestyle?

Test everything: Hold fast to the good. - 1 Thessalonians 5:21

The Alpha Initiative is arguably the most popular evangelistic programme in use in Britain's churches at present. Alpha's publications manager advises everyone "to do the course exactly as we've laid out for the first time – because we know it works." [Mark Elsdon-Drew, Christian Herald, 9:12:1995, p2] Well, a purely pragmatic approach to spiritual things is not scriptural and can be very dangerous. Of course I agree that "the natural desire of every Christian is to see souls saved" but I also agree that "at the same time we cannot simply close our eyes to all evangelistic outreaches trusting that they are biblically sound. There are two questions we must ask: What is the Ultimate aim, and what kind of gospel will be preached?" [Tricia Tillin, 'Networking: A Global Vision' in Mainstream Winter 1993, p3]. Referring to Matthew 23:15, Robert Bowman of the CRI, an evangelical discernment ministry, writes: "The Pharisees were extremely zealous in missionary work, but all they succeeded in doing was leading more people into their error. Zeal in witnessing or evangelising does not indicate that a religious group is God's people." [Robert Bowman, Orthodoxy and Heresy: A Guide to Doctrinal Discernment, 1993, p25] Today we might apply that to Jehovah's Witnesses for example.

Alpha certainly starts by preaching the gospel; the first three talks on video I focus on the person and work of Jesus Christ, and the three talks on video II which cover fundamental steps for new Christians, such as 'How can I be sure of my faith?', 'Why and how should I read the Bible?' and 'Why and how should I pray?' are all good. However, as the course progresses, some of the talks tend to wander off into lengthy accounts of Holy Trinity Brompton's experiences of the Toronto Blessing and associated ministries; novel exegeses of various Biblical passages common amongst pro-Toronto preachers; calls for unity despite truth and an over-emphasis on the Holy Spirit. All of these are less than helpful to potential Christians. Clearly the aim is to bring as many into God's Kingdom as possible but by the end of the course, I cannot help feeling that the Toronto Blessing may have been the greater beneficiary.

I
Alpha's connection with the Toronto Blessing

The Alpha Course has been used for approximately 16 years at HTB yet was virtually unknown elsewhere until Eleanor Mumford of the South-West London Vineyard church brought the Blessing back from the Toronto Airport Vineyard church in Canada to HTB, via Nicky Gumbel in May 1994.[1] In video III talk 9, Gumbel spends a substantial amount of time relating to Alpha participants exactly how it occured:

"We went to their house....where a group of leaders of their church was meeting....Ellie Mumford told us a little bit of what she had seen in Toronto....it was obvious that Ellie was just dying to pray for all of us....then she said 'Now we'll invite the Holy Spirit to come.' and the moment she said that, one of the people there was thrown, literally, across the room and was lying on the floor, just howling and laughing....making the most incredible noise....I experienced the power of the Spirit in a way I hadn't experienced for years, like massive electricity going through my body....One of the guys was prophesying. He was just lying there prohesying...." Gumbel returned to HTB where he apologised for being late for a meeting due to what had happened. Asked to close this meeting in prayer he says "I prayed 'Lord, thank you so much for all you are doing and we pray you'll send your Spirit' and I was just about to say 'in Jesus name, Amen' and go out the door when the Spirit came on the people who were in the room. One of them started laughing like a hyena...."

There are a few observations to make here. The first is the unquestioning acceptance by both groups of such unusual manifestations. Similarly the invocation of the Spirit was not queried. Secondly, I think it is pertinent to note that the Spirit came *before* the name of Jesus could be brought into the prayer. Thirdly, if one chap really was prophesying, then he was speaking directly to these people from God, and his words should have been heeded, tested and applied. But it seems they were completely ignored.

Later on in this account, and in talk 7, Gumbel compares the behaviour of these Toronto recipients, as do all Toronto leaders, to the 'drunken' behaviour of the apostles on the day of Pentecost. He says "they [the apostles] looked as though they were drunk; some of the manifestations were the same as that of a drunkard." Although this exegesis is a convenient explanation of the 'spiritual drunkenness' being seen at TB meetings, it is not the Biblical one, and has not been preached as such until now. The vast majority of the crowd were "bewildered", "amazed" and "perplexed" not because the apostles were showing "all the signs of inebriation" (talk 7), and which the passage itself nowhere indicates, but because *"we hear them declaring the wonders of God in our own tongues.*" (Acts 2:6-12) The crowd formed because of the sound of these tongues (v6) which were clear and easily understood. It was only a very small minority who accused the apostles of having had "too much wine" (v13), and there is no indication in the passage that, of such a large crowd, theirs was the *considered* judgement.

The result of the outpouring of the Holy Spirit on the day of Pentecost was a lengthy and powerful *sermon* which brought approximately 3000 people to faith in the Lord Jesus Christ almost immediately. Empowerment for service was the purpose of Pentecost and is the purpose of the Baptism in the Holy Spirit. The outpouring of the Holy Spirit was not given that we may lie on the floor on our backs with our feet in the air laughing like hyenas (talk 9). Gumbel's description of the antics that went on in the vestry of HTB after their invocation of the Spirit seems to me to bear no resemblance at all to what happened on the day of Pentecost.[2]

Yet Alpha participants are being taught all this as part of an evangelistic/ Christian Living course as though it is normal and desirable, with absolutely no mention made of the need to test the spirits (1 John 4:1-3), and at the end of this talk are prayed for, corporately, to receive it. Thus, they are initiated into the Toronto Blessing without a whimper of protest amongst them.

"I believe it is no coincidence that the present movement of the Holy Spirit [TB] has come at the same time as the explosion of the Alpha Courses. I think the two go together." [Nicky Gumbel, 'The Spirit and Evangelism', Renewal, May 1995, p15]

A. PROBLEMS WITH THE TORONTO BLESSING

1. The Blessing itself as experienced in meetings
Originated with Rodney Howard-Browne the 'Holy Ghost Bartender'.[3]

a) The nature of the blessing is experiential not Word-based, soulish not spiritual, ultimately self-seeking not God-seeking.[4]

b) The focus of worship is removed from the Father and the Son and placed instead on the Holy Spirit, contrary to John 14:26; 15:26; and 16:13-15. This is paralleled in the New Age movement's emphasis on the "coming of the Age of the Spirit (Aquarius) and consequently the demise of the Age of the Son (Pisces) and all who follow him." [David Forbes, Prophecy Today, N/D 1994, p12][5]

c) There is an over-emphasis on the power and – selective – gifts of the Holy Spirit (tongues, words of knowledge and prophecies [which are never tested against

Scripture, eg 1 Cor 14:29], and healing). The gift of discerning of spirits is noticeable by its absence.

d) The fruit of the Holy Spirit is seen to be tangible 'feelings' of love for Jesus etc. as produced by these experiences, rather than the life-long sanctification by the Word which is based on faith, not sight.[6] Once these 'feelings' wear off, the believer returns for a top-up. LSD works the same way.

e) The unbiblical practice of invoking the Holy Spirit: "If worshippers call out for the Spirit to descend upon them, the response may come from anywhere in the spirit world. The manifestations may well be spectacular, but counterfeit." [Clifford Hill, PT, S/O 1994, p12][7]

f) Many of the experiences/manifestations have no scriptural backing – except in the negative, and are more comparable with the works of the spirits of Eastern Mysticism and other unhealthy spirits than with the works of the Holy Spirit of God.[8] Describing his visit to the Toronto Airport Vineyard church, David Noakes says "The 'Toronto twitch' for example is explained as a power surge from the Holy Spirit. But Jesus did not go around having sudden power surges He couldn't control....many of the jerkings I saw in Toronto I would identify as being due to the spirits of voodoo. Some are due to spirits of martial arts. Some are due to spirits of lust. I would have no hesitation in declaring that animal noises do not come from the Holy Spirit. I have seen far too much of people manifesting animal noises and being delivered from the spirits of those very animals they are imitating." [David Noakes, Dealing with Poison in the Pot, audio tape CFCM 95/04, Jan 1995, side 1]

2. Theology underlying the Toronto Blessing
The Latter-Rain Movement.

Essentially a Christianised form of the secular theory of evolution which, beginning with the physical evolution of man from primitive life forms, will reach its culmination with the spiritual evolution of man into gods. This will be achieved through man's realisation of his 'Christ consciousness' or the 'Christ within' which, the New Age gurus tell us, is now beginning to occur as we move from the Age of Pisces to the Age of Aquarius. The whole thing is, of course, the belief in the lie Satan told Eve in the Garden of Eden (Genesis 3:4,5), yet it is finding its way into the Christian Church through the Latter-Rain's teaching on the 'Manifest-Sons-of-God', and the Word-of-Faith's teaching on the 'deification of man'. Latter-Rain also incorporates Kingdom-Now, Dominionism and Restorationism. These teachings are post-milleniallist and Triumphalist (i.e. they replace the Lord Jesus with the

Church) and include within them Replacement theology, which is a subtle form of anti-semitism.[9]

Latter-Rain doctrine was rejected as a heresy by the Assemblies of God in the 1950s, though accepted by other Pentecostal leaders such as William Branham (who was a direct influence on Paul Cain of the Kansas City Prophets), Oral Roberts, Kenneth Hagin (the so-called 'father' of the Word-of-Faith movement), and three out of the Fort Lauderdale Five who for many years published the widely read magazine 'New Wine'. Having bubbled along underground for a number of years Latter-Rain teachings are now resurfacing in various forms in many Charismatic churches on both sides of the Atlantic, in particular the Vineyard group of churches under the leadership of John Wimber.

The Kansas City Prophets are based at the Metro Vineyard church, the pastor of which is Mike Bickle whose recommendation of the Alpha Initiative can be seen in various editions of 'HTB in Focus: Alpha News', eg Aug 1995 p3.[10]

While there is no overt sign of Latter-Rain theology being taught on the Alpha course, the comment made by Sandy Millar at the beginning of video I: "Is it possible to attract people to the Christian faith today, in the sort of numbers that we need?" raises the question: "need" for *what*? Every unbeliever *needs* personal salvation, that is why the gospel is preached. But Sandy Millar did not say that. The paragraph of which that comment is a part, concentrates on the *Church's* need for members; for "new growth and new life" of the *Church*. Revival of the Church would be wonderful, but Scripture actually tells us that the opposite will happen before the return of the Lord Jesus (Matt 24:7-13; 2 Thess 2:3; 2 Tim 4:3-4 etc).[11] However, Restorationist/Kingdom-Now theology *needs* vast numbers of Christians so that the *Church* – united, militant and triumphant – can bring about God's kingdom on earth and then hand it over, restored to its Edenic state, to Jesus at his coming. Obviously that is a violent distortion of, amongst other scriptures, Acts 3:21, nevertheless it is an eschatology being taught and believed in many Charismatic fellowships today. Corporate not individual repentance is necessary to achieve the numbers required to form "God's endtime army that will march through the land to victory"; the ultimate aim of evangelism being "the establishing of the kingdom of God apart from Christ's return" [Mainstream, Summer 1994, p8]. Hopefully that is not what Sandy Millar meant. But in the light of so many deceptive doctrines around these days we cannot just dismiss, unexamined, the possibility that it might indeed mean what it seems to.

So one of my concerns is whether the TB, which is being experienced at HTB, can possibly be divorced from the Alpha Initiative. In view of the similarities of emphasis and content between the two, I'm not sure that it can, consequently I am concerned that in using the Alpha course as it stands, churches may inadvertently be introducing participants to the TB, with all it is a forerunner of, by the back door.[12]

[It is worthy of note that on 5th December 1995 the board of the Association of Vineyard churches removed the Toronto Airport Vineyard church from the Vineyard organisation. John Wimber felt that "the leaders of TAV have strong convictions which could not be reconciled with Vineyard values and the pastoral leadership and correction coming from the Vineyard Board."][13]

In common with the leadership of the Toronto Blessing, Alpha also promotes "unity" between Protestants and Roman Catholics, with no consideration, or perhaps realisation, of the irreconcileable doctrines of the two Churches. Thus another major concern is its trend towards Ecumenism.

II
Power Evangelism

"Where evangelism is integrally related to the supernatural power of the Holy Spirit" [Nicky Gumbel, Telling Others: The Alpha Initiative, p20].

Heavily influenced by the 'Signs and Wonders' ministry of John Wimber in the 1980s, power evangelism has been one of the preparation grounds for the Toronto Experience. It focuses on a pragmatic/experiential rather than a proclamatory/doctrinal approach to spreading the gospel. As such it tends to shift the focus away from the shed blood of Jesus on the cross and onto the supernatural works of the Holy Spirit carried out by men. This is the method of evangelism favoured by Alpha. [Telling Others pp21-24;29-31]

Dave Hunt, of Berean Call ministries in America, has written of power evangelism: "The over-emphasis upon and obsessive seeking after the *power* of the Spirit has caused many to forget that He is the 'Spirit of truth' who leads us into 'all *truth*', and the '*Holy* Spirit' who purifies our lives to God's glory.... The power that is manifested in miracles is more highly regarded than the power of truth to change hearts and deliver from bondage to sin....Sound doctrine loses its importance, while experiences are eagerly cultivated and made the basis for understanding God's will and even for interpreting His word....In contrast....Paul declared that 'the power' is in the preaching of the Cross (Rom 1:16; 1 Cor 1:18; Acts 14:1).... When Christians are more impressed with 'miracles' and 'results' than with adherence to sound doctrine the church is in serious trouble....We too often fail to make certain that those who are called upon 'to decide for Christ' fully understand the decision they are being asked to make....The emphasis throughout Scripture, and to which the church must return today, is clearly placed upon truth and *understanding* (1 John 5:20,21; John 8:43-45)." [Dave Hunt, Beyond Seduction: A Return to Biblical Christianity, 1987, pp77,78,238,257][14]

III
Alpha and the New Age

All of this heightened interest amongst Charismatic Christians in 'Signs and Wonders' and the supernatural experiences of the Toronto Blessing is a reflection of spiritual and cultural changes going on outside Christianity, of which New Age experiential mysticism is a predominant force.

Nicky Gumbel is aware of the paradigm shift from reason to experience: "In the Enlightenment reason ruled supreme and explanation led to experience. In the present transitional culture, with its 'pick-and-mix' worldview in which the New Age movement is a potent strand, experiences lead to explanation." [Nicky Gumbel, Telling Others, p19]

Post-Christian neo-mysticism is already so pervasive that virtually every non-Christian participant of Alpha – or any other evangelistic initiative – will to some degree reflect New Age thinking. In New Age philosophy "experiences lead to explanation" but in Christianity "If experience becomes relevant in certain areas it becomes relevant in applying the Word." [David Noakes, Dealing with Poison in the Pot, side 1] Yet, like the Toronto Experience, the thrust of Alpha is towards the experiental, and away from the written Word.

One pastor who has made use of the Alpha course writes: "One of the problems of proclaiming the gospel in a post-modern world is that culture itself warms much more readily to lifestyle than to doctrine. But the Christian lifestyle is not Christian faith....I am sure that many people are being converted through the Alpha course, but I have a suspicion that some of those people are being converted to a Christian lifestyle rather than to Christ." [Ian Lewis, 'The Alpha Course', Evangelicals Now, Dec 1995]

The two 'testimonies' given by Alpha participants at the beginning of the first Alpha video are prime examples of the above. There are certain basic elements one would expect to hear in a classic conversion testimony: The conviction of sin leading to repentance; the subsequent assurance of God's forgiveness and salvation through the death on the cross of Jesus Christ. Yet these are absent in any form in these 'testimonies'. As for the "new creation" Paul speaks of in 2 Cor 5:17, the good news would seem to be that there isn't one. Before she became a Christian, one of the participants recalls that she didn't want a personality change; she was happy with her life and saw no reason for change. "I now realise that my personality hasn't changed at all, but I feel that what has happened, *I'm actually getting more out of what I already had there,* and I think that's really God's work doing that."

A relationship with God is referred to, as is the experience of the baptism in the Holy Spirit, discovery of prayer, an interest in Bible reading, church-going, Christianity and what Alpha has done for them. However, Jesus and what *He* has done for them and a personal relationship with *Him* are not mentioned at all. Yet the Lord Jesus *is* the gospel. He *is* salvation. He *is* their new life. These things being so, how can He possibly be so completely overlooked in a basic conversion testimony? Adherents of false religions claim a relationship with God, and a prayer life, but they are not saved. Many church goers read their Bibles and have an interest in church and in Christianity, but they are not saved. Likewise, more compassion/ understanding at work, more patience, tolerance, confidence and deep feelings of contentment can equally well be produced by a sense of psychological wellbeing. Without the Cross they do not constitute salvation. The attempt by Gumbel to bring Jesus into the testimonies by asking exactly *what* had made these differences, was met with a blank look and the response: "Just the relationship that I've developed with God. Simple as that."

These testimonies seemed to me, as Ian Lewis suggests, only evidence of conversion to a Christian lifestyle, not to Christ. And when the "Christian lifestyle" is an endless round of 'blessings', supernatural 'experiences', spiritual 'parties' [see video talk 14] and 'play' times,[15] not noticeably different from non-christian spiritual experiences, then the transition from the counterfeit spirituality of the New Age to Christianity is really only one of degree, not kind. That being so I would echo the question of one evangelical minister who asked: "What is it they are converted to?" [Alan Morrison, 'How The Toronto Blessing Came To Town', in Evangelical Times, Nov 1994, p17]

IV
Evangelism or Christian Living?

"Scripture tells us that salvation comes through hearing the gospel, and I would expect any course aimed at non-christians to concentrate primarily on the facts of the gospel. The Alpha course deals with the basics of the gospel in two sessions....While these are unequivocally gospel presentations, the remainder of the course deals essentially with what may be described as Christian living....When we used an adapted version of the course in our church, non-christians were left behind by about the sixth week. They still had very fundamental questions about what

Christians believe, which were not answered by talking about how Christians live, and for this reason the course seemed more suited to people who have already made a commitment to Christ." [Ian Lewis, Evangelicals Now, Dec 1995]

In his introduction to the Alpha videos, Sandy Miller recognises that "most people need time in which to consider the most important claims they have ever had to face." It is ironic then that time is not given to Alpha participants in which to consider the person and work of Jesus Christ before they are rushed into the rest of the course.

A. THE HOLY SPIRIT WEEKEND
White Alpha training manual pp26-36, Video III talks 7-9

> "For a long time in the church the person and work of the Holy Spirit has been ignored – a greater concentration on the Father and the Son." [p26]
> "We live in the age of the Spirit." [p29]

These statements are misleading: Firstly, as an unbeliever or new Christian would not know the nature of the work of the Holy Spirit in relation to the Father and the Son, the statements effectively marginalise the first two sessions on the person and work of the Lord Jesus and serve to prepare the participant to accept unquestioningly anything that may occur during the weekend. Secondly, Christians have always referred to the period of time between the first and second advents as the age of Grace, or the Church age. That has not changed. Why then encourage, in today's precarious spiritual climate, the New Age concept of the Age of Aquarius (the spirit)?

Continuing his observations on the New Age Nicky Gumbel writes: "I have found on Alpha that those from an essentially enlightened background feel at home with the parts of the course which appeal to the mind, but often have difficulty in experiencing the Holy Spirit. Others coming from the New Age movement find that rational and historical explanations leave them cold, but at the weekend away they are on more familiar territory in experiencing the Holy Spiri.t" [Telling Others, p19]

But it is the "rational and historical explanations" of sessions 1 and 2 which are the essence of the gospel (Acts 2:22-41; 6:9-7:60; 8:26-38; 17:16-33) and which the unbeliever must grasp and accept with his *mind*, under the convicting and illuminating power of the Holy Spirit, if he is to repent and experience salvation in his heart (Romans 10:13,14). Moreover it is by the renewing of his mind that the Christian is transformed and made holy (Romans 12:1,2; see also Psalm 19:7-11) for without holiness he will not see God (Hebrews 12:14).

Nevertheless: "At the end of the course I send out questionnaires....if there is a change I ask when that change occurred. For many the decisive moment is the Saturday evening of the weekend." [Telling Others, p120] This is the time when Gumbel invites the Holy Spirit to come and participants are filled with the Spirit. [Telling Others, pp117,120,123; Blue Alpha training manual p18]

I find this extremely worrying. The "decisive moment" should surely be the point at which a person steps over from eternal death to eternal life through the *conversion* experience (John 3:16; 5:24; Romans 10:9,10,13 and other refs). But most of the testimonies in 'Telling Others' seem to confuse the experience of conversion with the experience of baptism in the Holy Spirit.

But is this surprising when Gumbel himself seems to treat conversion as a preliminary to the main event? The breath of new life into a repentant sinner is taught in talk 7, but Gumbel does not make it clear that this happens at *conversion* (2Cor 5:17). Rather, he suggests this is due to a second experience: the baptism in the Spirit. References to Isaiah 61:1-3 and to Samson's freedom "from the ropes that bound him", for example, are applied to the Holy Spirit, despite the fact that in Luke 4:16-21 Jesus is quoting the Isaiah passage with reference to himself. It is the shed blood of Jesus that frees us from the things that bind us (John 8:32-36; Gal 5:1; Rev 1:5). Likewise, in discussing Paul's conversion in talk 9, the emphasis is placed, not on Paul's meeting with Jesus Christ, but on his subsequent baptism in the Spirit.

On preparing participants for baptism in the Holy Spirit, leaders are advised to "take time to sort out difficulties of understanding, belief and assurance; lead to Christ." [Blue Alpha training manual p17; Telling Others pp116-120] To say that to be unsaved is a "difficulty of understanding, belief and assurance" is, I would suggest, an understatement of some magnitude! Coupled with the unbiblical practice of invoking the Holy Spirit at this point in the course, it is necessary to ask whether it truly is the baptism in the Holy Spirit these participants are experiencing. The ramifications, if they are not, are obvious and terrible.[16]

The following testimony is an alarming example of the confusion between conversion and baptism in the Holy Spirit, but it is by no means the only one:

"....[M]y wife encouraged me to read an article in a magazine about the Alpha course at HTB. What had stuck in my mind was how the work of the Holy Spirit was described as of paramount importance. I knew in my heart I had to have his power in my life at any cost. So I....enrolled on the course and focused on the weekend where the work of the Holy Spirit is discussed....Never mind the weeks of pre-med, I just had to get into the operating theatre....I looked at the order of play, saw that the third session on 'How can I be filled with the Spirit' (which I identified as the main one) was at 4:30pm and simply hung on like a marathon runner weaving his way up the finishing straight with nothing but the finishing tape as the focus of his attention....the prize was so near but we were getting there so slowly. I literally wanted to scream out 'Do it now! Do it now! I can't hold out any longer'. I'm not exaggerating when I say I was in agony. Then Nicky Gumbel invited the Spirit to come and oh, the relief..." [Interview in Renewal, Oct 1995, p16; Telling Others pp36-37]

Once that extraordinary testimony has sunk in, a few things become apparent: firstly, as with the testimonies on the video the basic elements of a conversion testimony are missing. In fact the gospel of Christ is referred to here as "pre-med" in which, the participant plainly states, he had no interest. Secondly, not only did Nicky Gumbel not seek to correct the focus of this participant from the Holy Spirit onto the Lord Jesus where it rightly belongs, and ensure he had actually been saved, but he also gave the testimony a prominent place in 'Telling Others' as a witness and example to others. One Sunday following this experience, the Holy Spirit supposedly directed this man to a Vineyard church sixty miles away from his home in order that a long-standing problem with his back might be healed. Why a *Vineyard* church? And why so far from home? Was there not one single church of any kind nearer than that? Did the Holy Spirit guide Lydia and the Philippian jailor sixty miles away to the fellowship in, say, Thessalonica? Of course not. They fellowshipped with other believers in Philippi, their home town, and if they were sick they called on the elders in that church to pray for them. It is no different for us. Also, Dominionism and Triumphalism are evident in the last three paragraphs of the testimony as given in Renewal [p17]. This participant is now a helper on Alpha courses at HTB.

In talk 8, Gumbel says "When we come to Christ the first thing the Holy Spirit wants to do is to assure us of that relationship, and that we are totally, totally forgiven." Although he continues "the Holy Spirit witnesses to our spirit that we are children of God", all the subsequent examples focus on soulish (ie tangible) feelings and experiences. The testimony at the beginning of video I in which "a sensation of energy.... as if I had 5000 volts thrashing through my body" is seen to be the Holy Spirit's assurance of conversion, is only one example of the results of such teaching. Experiences of this kind can be, and are, produced by any spirit wanting access to a believers life. I am not convinced they come from the *Holy* Spirit. We can know we are "totally, totally forgiven" because the Bible says so, and it is to the Word that the Holy Spirit leads us, and through which He sanctifies us. Praise God that our assurance of salvation does *not* rest on our unreliable feelings and experiences!

The misuse of Ephesians 5:18-20 and Revelation 22:17 in talk 8, in order to initiate Alpha participants into the TB is inexcusable. In the Ephesians passage, Paul is not commanding the believers to experience a second Pentecost, but is rebuking them for behaving like pagans and unbelievers. Verse 18 is a *contrast* not a *comparison* between the fruit produced by the Holy Spirit and the fruit produced by the sinful nature. It is a call by Paul, not for *baptism* (ie empowerment for service) but for *sanctification*, for some evidence of the *fruit* of the Holy Spirit in their lives which at that point was seriously lacking.

The passage in Revelation has absolutely nothing whatsoever to do with Pentecost (the Holy Spirit is hardly going to invoke Himself) and everything to do with the physical return of the Lord Jesus Christ at the end of the age.

Though the prayer at the end of these talks includes repentance, the gospel talks are not at this point uppermost in participants minds, and the corporate request "inviting the Holy Spirit to come and fill us" is then made by all in the room.

The content of these three talks overlaps to such an extent that they could quite easily have been combined into one address. In fact each aspect of the Holy Spirit's work could have been included in the relevant sections of the other talks. The Spirit's conviction of sin in an unbeliever, for example, fits in with talks 2 and 3 (sessions 1 and 2); assurance of salvation in talk 4; teaching believers the Word in talk 5; enabling believers to pray in talk 6; producing fruit and empowering us for service in talk 15 and so on.[17]

Through these talks the focus has thus shifted very definitely from the Cross of Christ to the power of the Spirit.

For Gumbel's teaching on 'Unity in the Family' in this talk see section *F. WHAT ABOUT THE CHURCH?* below.

B. HOW CAN I RESIST EVIL?
Session 9 White Alpha training manual pp39-45 Video IV Talk 10

In section II of this session Satan's tactics are listed: Destroys; blinds eyes; causes doubt; tempts; accuses.

All of these Gumbel applies to the area of Christian behaviour. Deception, the tactic focusing on belief is omitted. This oversight can be deadly. Deception concerning doctrine is Satan's most powerful weapon against the Church and new Christians need to be made aware just how practised Satan is at deceiving Christians through false doctrines and false spiritual experiences.[18]

When asked by His disciples what would be the signs of His return, Jesus' first words in response were "Take heed that no man deceive you" (Matt 24:4, also 24:5;10;11;23-25). A great deal of the content of the letters to the New Testament churches were warnings against being deceived by heresies and false teachers (eg 2 Cor 11:3; Gal 1:6-9;3:1-5; 2 Thess 2:1-3; 1 Tim 4:1; 2 Peter 2:1-3; 1 John 2:24; 1 John 4:1-6; 2 John 7-11; the list of references is endless).

One of the main factors in the unquestioning acceptance of the Toronto Experience is that we believers simply do not realise we are capable of being deceived; that not everything that is supernatural necessarily comes from God, despite many cases in Scripture where supernatural happenings originate in the occult (Exodus 7:11-12; Acts 8:9-11; Acts 16:16-18; 2 Thess 2:9; Rev 13:1-3,11-15).

Nicky Gumbel points out in this talk that occult activity "always comes under the guise of something good". The Toronto Blessing is seen as "something good". How strange then that neither he nor anyone else at HTB thought to test the Toronto spirit before accepting it and then passing it on to everyone else. [19]

A solid grounding in essential doctrine, the cultivation of the Berean spirit (Acts 17:11) and a familiarity with eschatology are vital in combating deception in these last days. None of these is experiential. All of them require application of the mind. All of them have been in short supply in the Charismatic movement to date.

C. HOW DOES GOD GUIDE US?
Session 10 White Alpha training manual pp46-51 Video IV Talk 11

The "Guiding Spirit" and "more unusual ways" of guidance referred to in this talk, especially guidance by angels, need *thorough* testing against Scripture in today's religious climate in which false prophets and occult 'spirit guides' masquerading as angels of light abound.

For millenia spiritists have been mediums for familiar spirits and divining spirits. Now, as New Agers are regarding themselves as 'channelers' for their 'spirit guides', so too there is an alarming trend beginning to emerge amongst experience orientated Christians, mainly in America, to talk of their 'angel guides'. [20]

A testimony in 'HTB in Focus, Alpha News', Aug 1995, in which Jesus is referred to as "a guiding light" (p14), is just an inkling of what may be to come.

D. WHY AND HOW SHOULD WE TELL OTHERS?
Session 11 White Alpha training manual pp52-57 Video IV Talk 12

See comments in **II Power Evangelism** above: *Page7.*

E. DOES GOD HEAL TODAY?
Session 12 White Alpha training manual pp58-62 Video V Talk 13

During this talk Nicky Gumbel tells Alpha participants of the visit by John Wimber to HTB in 1982 to demonstrate God's power to heal. He says: "John

Wimber then said 'We've had words of knowledge.' These are supernatural revelations, things that they couldn't have known otherwise about the conditions of people in the room....specific details were given, accurately describing the conditions....as the list was responded to, the level of faith in the room was rising." Gumbel says that he still felt "cynical and hostile" until the following evening when he was prayed for: "So they prayed for the Spirit to come....I felt something like 10,000 volts going through my body....The American had a fairly limited prayer. He just said 'more power'....it was the only thing he ever prayed. I can't remember him ever praying anything else....Now we've seen many kinds of these manifestations of the Spirit on the weekends....these manifestations....and the physical healings themselves are not the important thing....the fruit of the Spirit....these are the things that matter, the fruit that comes from these experiences. So we began to realise that God heals miraculously...."

Bearing in mind that his warning in talk 10 about occult activity disguising itself as something good used healing as an example, it is surprising that Gumbel gives no indication here that he or anyone else attending the meeting tested the spirits to ensure that everything came from the *Holy* Spirit. Gumbel surely knows that, like healings, words of knowledge and prophesies can also come from an occult source. That they are factual or come to pass does not prove their source is God. They could equally well come from a spirit of divination (see Acts 16:16-19), and if they do, they and the person uttering them must be rejected (see Deut 13:1-11). I am not saying that this is necessarily the case here, but everything claiming supernatural origin must be tested, no matter how renowned the speaker might be. The fact that the "level of faith" rose in response to the accuracy of the words given merely indicates the extent of the gullibility of the congregation, not the source of the words, or the healings which may have followed.

To hear the prayer "more power" so many years before the TB where, along with "more Lord" it has become a kind of mantra, startled me. With no mention of the name of the Lord Jesus, this American gave Gumbel no indication of who he was praying to or what sort of "power" he was praying for. Worse still, Gumbel did not ask him. A prayer of that kind is an open invitation to any spirit anywhere to do anything it chooses in the life of the recipient.

And, of course, the fruit of the Holy Spirit does not come from "these experiences" but from the daily sanctification by the Holy Spirit through obedience to the Word (John 14:15;21;23-26; 15:1-7;10;14-15). Once again Alpha participants are not being warned of the very serious dangers of accepting anything and everything from anyone and everyone. So they will walk out of the cocoon of Alpha and straight into the path of the *enemy the devil [who] prowls around like a roaring lion looking for someone to devour"* (1 Peter 5:8).

Ian Lewis was concerned regarding this talk that "The emphasis on technique rather than faith in these areas seems to me to be less than helpful, and fails to address these issues in their true biblical context." [Ian Lewis, Evangelicals Now, 1995 – see Appendix 1]

It is however good to see Gumbel's teaching on the difference between the Kingdom of God pre- and post-Jesus' return in which he states that "complete healing has not yet arrived. We can still suffer from sickness in this life. Not everyone is healed. Even in the ministry of Jesus not everyone was healed." No sign of Latter-Rain or Word-of-Faith teaching there!

F. WHAT ABOUT THE CHURCH?
Session 13 White Alpha training manual pp63-68 Video V Talk 14

1. Romanism

"The Alpha course is....adaptable across tradition and denominations....I know of its uses in Catholic....churches" [Martin Cavender in Telling Others].

Adaptable in what sense exactly?

Alpha's publications manager advises that, while presentation of the material can be adapted to suit, the content should be followed exactly. (He makes particular reference to the weekend dealing with the Holy Spirit in this respect) [Christian Herald, 9:12:1995].

If the content of the course teaches the fundamental historical and theological facts and doctrines of the Christian faith as recorded in Scripture, then, having tested and proved that to be so, any Protestant church using Alpha could follow the course exactly. But could a Catholic church do that?

In talk 5 Gumbel teaches from 2 Timothy 3:16 that the Bible is useful for teaching, correcting and rebuking, which of course it is. "It's how we know if something is wrong. How do we know that what Jehovah's Witnesses believe is not right? We have to put it alongside the Bible – also the Moonies – and test it. And if you do that, I think you'll find it's not consistent with the teaching of the New Testament."

Protestantism teaches salvation by faith alone through grace alone; Romanism adds to the cross mans' good works, and a whole host of other non-Biblical doctrines such as purgatory, penance, transubstantiation, indulgences, prayers to/ for the dead/saints, papal infallibility, Mariolatry, sacerdotal mediation etc, etc. So if we "put [Romanism] alongside the Bible" we can see that "it's not consistent with the teaching of the New Testament." Romanism falls into the category described by Paul as 'Judaisers' (Philippians 3:2-11), who add to the gospel of Christ the works of men (Gal 3:1-25; Ephesians 2:4-10; Heb 9:24-10:1-18). Romanism bears not a little resemblance to the teachings and works of the Pharisees so scathingly denounced by Jesus in Matthew 23:1-28. It is a false religion that will *never* relinquish a single one of its unscriptural tenets to Protestantism.

Nevertheless, in in section II of this talk and in talk 8, Gumbel teaches Alpha participants that the differences between Protestants and Catholics are "totally insignificant compared to the things that unite us....we need to unite around the death of Jesus, the resurrection of Jesus; the absolute essential things at the core of the Christian faith on which we are all agreed. We need to give people liberty to disagree on the things which are secondary." I wholeheartedly agree with the last sentence but that is not the issue here. It is on the *essentials* that Protestants and Catholics do not have unity. That was the whole point of the Protestant Reformation. Every one of the Canons anathematizing Protestant doctrine in the Catholic Council of Trent in the 16th Century still stands. In fact unscriptural doctrines are still being added to the Roman belief system; the doctrine that Mary is co-redemptress with Christ for example, is a recent addition and is not by any stretch of the imagination, a secondary issue.

Discussing the price of unity in the Church, Bishop Ryle wrote: "Our noble Reformers bought the truth at the price of their own blood, and handed it down to us. Let us take heed that we do not basely sell it for a mess of pottage, under the specious names of unity and peace." [Warnings to the Churches, 1877, p128]

Still Gumbel says: "We need to unite....there has been some comment which is not helpful to unity. Let us drop that and get on. It is wonderful that the movement of the Spirit will always bring churches together. He is doing that right across the denominations and within the traditions....we are seeing Roman Catholics coming now....Nobody is suspicious of anybody else....People are no longer 'labelling' themselves or others. I long for the day when we drop all these labels and just regard ourselves as Christians with a commission from Jesus Christ." [Renewal, May 1995, p16]

'Labelling' is a sociological term. In this inclusivist age in which truth is believed to be relative (note the convenient lack of relativism of that particular 'truth'!) it is used, not to define the labellee, but to discredit the labeller. Used in this sense it is as ridiculous to "drop all labels and just regard ourselves [Protestants and Catholics] as Christians" as it would be to refuse to label the jam-pot 'jam' and the marmalade-pot 'marmalade'. A vast number of Catholics have not heard the gospel in their churches and Protestants cannot just assume they are saved.

'Adaptability' of the Alpha course to include Catholics, not necessarily to convert them, is referred to in Alpha as 'unity', and I am concerned that Alpha is contributing – albeit unintentionally – to the undoing of the Protestant Reformation through the promulgation of Ecumenism disguised as Christian Unity.[21]

2. Unity and false doctrine/teachers

Unity is the keyword of the church growth movement who would agree with Nicky Gumbel that "a disunited church, squabbling and criticising makes it very hard for the world to believe." [Renewal, May 1995, p16] Consequently "we make it a rule on Alpha never to criticize another denomination, another Christian church or a Christian leader." [Telling Others, p114; and this talk, section II] "Actually we must stop judging one another." [The Impact of Toronto, p83]

Yet there are times when failure to "criticize" – or rather to rebuke and correct (2 Tim 3:16; 4:2-5) – is actually to be disobedient to the Word of God. Although in talk 5 Gumbel only applied the rebuking and correcting to Christian behaviour, it also applies to false teaching.

We must certainly not judge one anothers sins or their hearts (eg Matt 7:1-5), or their personalities, but we *are* to test all teachings, prophecies and practices against Scripture and *judge* whether they are true or false (1 Cor 2:15;16; 1 Thess 5:21; 1 John 4:1). Far from gullibly swallowing everything we are told, however respected the teacher, believers are to test all that passes for doctrine (Acts 17:11), to correct and rebuke those in error – for *their* sake! – (2 Tim 4:2-5) and to disassociate from those who continue to preach false doctrine (Romans 16:17,18; 2 John 7-11). Jesus, Paul and John all named publicly those who opposed the truth publicly (Matt 23:1-39; Gal 2:11-14; 2 Tim 2:14-26; Titus 1:10-14; 3 John 1:9,10 [Matt 18:15-17 applies to private disagreements]), and we must do the same for the sake of those believers following them.[22] Participants of Alpha are not being taught this.

As with the JWs, Moonies and Romanism so with less obvious heresies and false teachings operating *within* mainstream Christianity. They are "not consistent with the teaching of the New Testament" – or the Old, and Gumbel is right: "All these heresies, all these cults were around in a very similar form in New Testament times and they [the apostles] dealt with them and the answers are there in the Bible." Today however, instead of recognising that, just like the heresies of the 1st Century and the JWs of the 20th Century, these groups are preaching "a Jesus other than the Jesus we preached", we, like the Corinthians to whom Paul was writing, are welcoming them with open arms.

According to Ephesians 4:3-6 Christian unity comes through our being baptised through one Spirit into "one Lord, one faith, one baptism; one God and Father of all." In John 17 Jesus only prayed for the unity of all believers (vs11,23) after He had prayed for the sanctification of His disciples by the *truth*, which He immediately went on to define – for our benefit, not for His Father's – as God's Word (v17). Shortly before this Jesus had told His disciples that one of the works of the Holy Spirit was to guide them into all truth (John 16:13-15). So the Holy Spirit unites believers/churches (John 17:23) through God's written Word (John 16:13; 17:17). As He does not contradict Himself there can therefore, only be unity *within* biblical truth/sound doctrine; there cannot be unity *despite* biblical truth/sound doctrine. Those who do not preach or follow the truth, have *broken* the unity of the believers.[23]

Unity is also essential to Latter-Rain doctrine, to enable the incarnation of Christ into His physical body (the Church), because He cannot incarnate a divided body, so that the Church may become the 'manifest sons-of-God'. But Latter-Rain is a "different gospel" (Gal 1:6-7) with a faulty eschatology which is insinuating itself into Charismatic fellowships these days; one of its most successful routes being the Toronto Blessing.[24]

It is vital that we *"earnestly contend for the faith which was once delivered unto the saints"* (Jude 3). If not, we may find ourselves, and those new believers whom we have nurtured, part of the Apostate Church. This is very serious. Christian/Church unity is also essential to the New Age goal of global unity. The Apostate church is the thin end of this wedge; the middle of which is religious inclusivism/syncretism; the wide end being the one-world religion under the control of the False Prophet during the reign of the Antichrist and his one-world government.

3. The Parable of the Party

In section IV, Gumbel says the Church, though God's Holy Temple, so often loses "the sense of the presence of God in its midst". He is making reference here to the Sunday meetings of believers rather than to the Church as the body of Christ and uses the parable of the Prodigal Son to explain that Sunday services should be like a 'party'. "Jesus was saying that....the Church is like....a feast and a celebration, and at a party everyone has a good time. There's fun, there's laughter....Why shouldn't there be laughter at the biggest party of all? And that's what we're seeing today, laughter and fun, and people getting drunk – not with wine, Paul says 'don't get drunk with wine – be filled with the Spirit, [but see my comments on Ephesians 5, p8]....Come to a party where you can get drunk on God....I was at a party like that last night. It was a whole load of church leaders, and we invited the Spirit to come....It was a party thrown by the Holy Spirit.... It was a fun place to be. The Church is meant to be a party.... That's the sort of picture – a Holy Temple."

David Noakes writes of his visit to the Toronto Airport Vineyard church: "Luke 15 was brought to us as a Scripture that tells us in these days that God is a God of parties. God is partying. Lots of jokes from a great big fun God. I don't know what sort of God that is. I haven't found that God in the Bible. My God is a consuming fire. He's a God of grace and compassion and love but I don't trifle with the God I know. I don't go partying with balloons and fun and jokes and things. When I find God weeping over the state of the Church I can't go around with balloons in my hand....and yet the Scripture is misused and taken to say this is God; a God of parties. I understand that Scripture as a God of mercy and compassion and forgiveness, always ready to receive back the repentant sinner. I find nothing about God partying. Yes, the celebration was to indicate the greatness of His love and the greatness of the restoration, but it was used [at Toronto] for a totally false purpose." [David Noakes, Dealing with Poison in the Pot, side 1]

The Church will celebrate the marriage feast of the Lamb when the Lord Jesus returns, but I find no references to "fun" or "parties" anywhere in Scripture, except in denunciation. In 1 Corinthians 10:1-11 for example, Paul reminds the Corinthians of God's anger against His people Israel in the wilderness because they did not patiently wait for Moses to return from the mountain, but built themselves a golden calf and held a festival; eating, drinking and indulging in revelry (Exodus 32:1-10). It made no difference to God that the festival was "to the Lord" (v5), or that they had all been freed from Egypt and had all been partakers of the "spiritual rock that accompanied them, and that rock was Christ" (1 Cor 10:14). They were still forbidden entrance to the promised land. Paul's point here is to compare the Christian life with the wilderness experience of the people of Israel. We may have left Egypt but we have yet to enter the promised land. Until Jesus returns and we attend the marriage feast of the Lamb, there is no place for "parties" or "festivals"; not even "to the Lord". Rather, *"....true worshippers....worship the Father in spirit and truth, for they are the kind of worshippers the Father seeks. God is spirit and His worshippers must worship in spirit and in truth"* (John 4:23,24).[25]

In the last section of this presentation, Gumbel teaches participants that the Church is the Bride of Christ. He asks: "Are we worthy to be the bride?" Cleansed, restored and forgiven by the blood of Jesus on the Cross, Gumbel says the Church is to be "holy and without blemish". She is to be "in love with Jesus....One of the things we've found in the last few weeks as people have experienced the power of the Spirit....we're falling in love with Jesus Christ". Well, feelings of being "in love with Jesus" do not make us holy. Experiences of "the power of the Spirit" do not make us holy. Going to "spiritual parties" to get "spiritually drunk" that we may lose control of our minds and bodies is certainly not the way to holiness. It is through the renewing of our minds, through self-control, through obedience to the truth and through our hope in Jesus Christ that we are made holy (Romans 12:1,2; Heb 12:14-17; 1 Peter 1:13-2:3).

How true the prophesy uttered in Azusa Street in 1906 has proved to be: "In the last days three things will happen in the Great Pentecostal Movement: There will be an over-emphasis on power, rather than on righteousness; there will be an over-emphasis on praise, to a God they no longer pray to; there will be an over-emphasis on the gifts of the Spirit, rather than on the lordship of Christ."

Are we worthy to be the bride? I don't think we are.

G. HOW CAN I MAKE THE MOST OF THE REST OF MY LIFE?
Session 14 White Alpha training manual pp69-71 Video V Talk 15

I am aware that this title is designed to appeal to the enthusiasm of new converts to continue along the Christian way, but its similarity to the Word-of-Faith's prosperity/health and wealth label, which is very much a 'what's-in-it-for-me-in-this-life?' gospel, suggests a way of life that bears no resemblance whatsoever to true discipleship.

However, the content of the session belies its title, focusing on Romans 12:1-21, and reminding participants that as "God did not spare His own Son, so it is just a little thing for us to give our lives to God as a living sacrifice."

V

Eschatology and Church History

The basics of Christian discipleship include an eager expectation of and preparation for the return of our Lord Jesus (Matt 24:1-chap 25:46; 1 and 2 Thess; Rev 1-22). However God's cry for his people Israel in Hosea 4:6-14 "My people are destroyed from lack of knowledge", applies no less to His Church, as evidenced in the unquestioning acceptance amongst many Christians of every new 'shepherd', 'prophet', 'doctrine' or spiritual 'experience' that comes along. If new disciples are to finish the race they, and we, have begun (Acts 20:22-24; 1 Cor 9:24; Gal 5:7-10; 2 Tim 4:6-8; Heb 12:1-3), then at least some instruction in eschatology and relevant elements in Church history (persecutions, heresies, the Protestant Reformation) would be useful.

VI
CONCLUSION

I believe we have a grave responsibility in these spiritually perilous times to ensure that we do not introduce any teaching into our fellowships which does not accord with the written Word of God. Surely any system of instruction/evangelism should be thoroughly tested in the light of Scripture by church leaders before being used as a basis for teaching.

I don't think we can compare one sermon given by a visiting speaker to a fellowship of believers, who are mature enough in the faith to be able to test what is being said and sieve out the dross while holding on to the good, with an entire teaching course of 14-15 talks given to non-Christians who are completely ignorant of the Word of God. Also, while we do not know what the visiting preacher will say until he says it, the Alpha videos and training manuals tell us exactly what will be taught. If we run the course from the videos, we have to use everything that is on them; fast-forwarding the bits we may not agree with is not an option. It is not enough to say any errors can be corrected in discussion groups afterwards. Proverbs 22:6 tells us to **"Train a child in the way he should go, and when he is old he will not depart from it."** This applies to children in the faith as much as it does to children in age, and it concerns belief no less than behaviour. We would not deliberately teach our children something we knew was wrong with the excuse that we could correct it later. If we know some teaching is wrong before we teach it, why teach it? Why not just teach what is right to begin with? It may only be part of Alpha's teaching which does not accord with Scripture, but I would say with Paul: **A little yeast works through the whole batch of dough.** (Gal 5:9) Though Paul is talking here of the yeast of the law, the yeast of lawlessness is just as damaging. Ultimately it is not the leaders of Alpha or anyone else who will stand responsible before God for the spiritual health of those nurtured in our fellowships, but we ourselves.

Every Christian and every fellowship is able to witness to the gospel. Many fellowships create their own evangelistic courses under the guidance of the Holy Spirit. It should not be necessary to rely on the methods and techniques of another fellowship when we have all the instruction and teaching material we need in Scripture, all the experience we need in each of our relationships with the Lord Jesus and are each empowered by the Holy Spirit to go and do it. Bearing in mind the tendency of Church evangelism today to preach a God of love but not a God of holiness or judgement, and thus to emphasise what we are saved *to* at the expense of what we are saved *from* – part of what Yacov Prasch has called a 'Re-definition' rather than a 'Re-contextualisation' of the Christian gospel [Yacov Prasch, The

Anglican/Evangelical Dilemma, audio tape LC24(e), 1996, Banner Ministries], it is surely necessary that in any evangelistic outreach we undertake, we ensure that:

A. Non-believing participants have fully understood the meaning of the cross and are saved (sessions 1 and 2) before propelling them into a course on Christian Living (sessions 3-14).

B. Converts are fully aware of their *conversion* experience and are becoming stable in their daily relationship with the Lord Jesus before thrusting them into the baptism of the Holy Spirit, for which they are not yet ready and which could allow into their lives the influence of an alien spirit through ground given, albeit unintentionally.

C. Participants understand the different nature of the work of each person in the Trinity.

D. The fruit of the Holy Spirit, and His convicting and sanctifying work in a believers life is not submerged beneath the gifts and the power of the Holy Spirit.

E. Participants are taught to proceed from the Word to experience, not from experience to the Word. i.e. that they – and we – know the difference between the experience of the Christian life as the daily application of and obedience to God's written Word, and the supernatural experiences (plural) so characteristic of the Toronto Blessing.

F. Participants understand that deception regarding doctrine and supernatural phenomena has always been Satan's main weapon against the Church and that knowing and standing fast in the Word is our weapon of defence, as it was for Jesus (Matt 4:1-11).

G. Participants are taught to become Bereans (Acts 17:11) able to test everything against Scripture for themselves, not relying on leaders, who are not infallible (e.g. Gal 2:11-14), to do their thinking and living for them. This has been the particular failing of the 'Heavy Shepherding' movement within some Charismatic fellowships during the last 20 years; it has failed to produce Scripture-literate, discerning Christians. Also we must teach them to keep their eyes fixed on Jesus, *the author and perfecter of our faith* (Heb 12:2), and teach them to *earnestly contend for the faith which was once for all delivered unto the saints* (Jude 3).

H. For churches that do use the Alpha Course I would also recommend revision of the booklist on pp72-75 of the white Alpha training manual as it tends to display a bias towards writers sympathetic to the Vineyard/Toronto Experience/Restorationist persuasion, while omitting other sound and more obvious choices in several of the sessions. While there are many good books on healing, for example, 2 of the 3 books listed in this section are written by John Wimber. At least two of the recommended authors for session 2 do not agree with the Biblical view of hell, but prefer the idea of annihilation. And while 'Chasing the Dragon', may be an interesting autobiography, it does not claim to be a text book on the Holy Spirit. It should not be too difficult for any church to compile its own recommended reading list.

In 1877 Bishop Ryle wrote: "The Lord Jesus Christ declares, '*I* will build My Church'....Ministers may preach, and writers may write, but the Lord Jesus Christ alone can build. And except He builds, the work stands still....Sometimes the work goes on fast, and sometimes it goes on slowly. Man is frequently impatient, and thinks that nothing is doing. But man's time is not God's time. A thousand years in His sight are but as a single day. The great builder makes no mistakes. He knows what He is doing. He sees the end from the beginning. He works by a perfect, unalterable and certain plan" [J.C. Ryle 'The True Church' in Warnings to the Churches, 1877, pp13-14].

And they continued steadfastly in the apostles' doctrine and fellowship, and in breaking of bread, and in prayers....Praising God, and having favour with all the people. And the Lord added to the church daily such as should be saved. (Acts 2:42,47.

NOTES

1. HTB in FOCUS: ALPHA NEWS, Aug 1995 p9.
   See also Wallace Boulton, ed., THE IMPACT OF TORONTO, 1995 pp20-24.
2. See Richard Smith, SPIRITUAL DRUNKENNESS: ITS CAUSES, CONSEQUENCES AND CURES, audio tape, I.T.S., 1994/22.
3. Ed Tarkowski, THE LAUGHING PHENOMENA: ITS HISTORY AND POSSIBLE EFFECTS ON THE CHURCH, 1995, pp5-6.
   See also Stephen Sizer, 'Toronto: Cautions' in EVANGELICALS NOW, Nov 1994, p9. And Alan Morrison, A DIFFERENT GOSPEL: THE ORIGIN AND PURPOSE OF THE "TORONTO BLESSING", 1994, and A PLAGUE IN THE LAND: GOD'S PURPOSES IN THE "TORONTO BLESSING", (video tapes showing footage of Rodney Howard-Browne in action at Benny Hinn's meeting, 1991, and at Kenneth Copeland's meeting, 1993).
4. See, for example: Jack Dunnigan, 'A Shoppers Paradise' in PROPHESY TODAY, Nov/Dec 1994, pp10-11. Johannes Facius, 'Laugh? I Nearly Cried' in PROPHESY TODAY, May/June 1995, pp24-26. Intercessors for Britain, 'Soul or Spirit?' in TORONTO: BLESSING OR BLIGHT? 1995, pp6-7.
5. This parallel is widely noted; see, for example: David Noakes, 'REVIEW OF LEADERSHIP CONSULTATION HELD AT BAWTRY IN JANUARY 1995, (Leadership Consultation on the current situation in the Charismatic churches), audio tape CFCM 95/07, Mar 1995, side 1.
6. See for example, Chris Hand, FALSE FRUIT, audio tape IFB/192, July 1995, side 1.
7. See also David Pawson, IS THE BLESSING BIBLICAL? 1995, pp60-63. And David Noakes, audio tape CFCM 95/07, side 1.
8. See for example: Reachout Trust, GODS OF THE NEW AGE, video tape, 1988. Mick Brown, 'Unzipper Heaven, Lord' in SUNDAY TELEGRAPH MAGAZINE, Oct 1994, pp26-30 and subsequent interview 'What Happened Next? Toronto and the Telegraph Reporter' in EVANGELICALS NOW, Feb 1995, pp1,
   Nader Mikhaiel, SLAYING IN THE SPIRIT: THE TELLING WONDER, 2nd edition, 1995.
   Philip Foster, SUGGESTIBILITY, HYSTERIA AND HYPNOSIS, 1996.
9. Refer to David Forbes, THE INFLUENCE OF LATTER-RAIN TEACHING ON THE CHARISMATIC MOVEMENT, audio tape CFCM 95/03.
   Also Tricia Tillin, RESTORATIONISM, TORONTO AND THE LATTER-RAIN, 2 audio tapes, 1994.
   For teachings of the New Age see, for example, Constance Cumbey, THE HIDDEN DANGERS OF THE RAINBOW: THE NEW AGE MOVEMENT AND OUR COMING AGE OF BARBARISM, 1983. For comparison of New Age with Latter-Rain teachings see, for example, Ed Tarkowski, THE LAUGHING PHENOMENA, pp25-40.
10. For information on the Kansas City prophets refer to various audio tapes available from Banner Ministries. For information on the Word-of-Faith movement see, for example, Hank Hanegraaff, CHRISTIANITY IN CRISIS, 1993. Also, various audio tapes available from Banner Ministries.
11. See for example, Intercessors For Britain, REVIVAL OR SURVIVAL? 1995.
12. For other relevant information on the Toronto Blessing see: Clifford Hill, ed., BLESSING THE CHURCH? 1995. Stanley Jebb, NO LAUGHING MATTER, 1995.
    Leigh Belcham, TORONTO: THE BABY OR THE BATHWATER? 1995.
    Bill Randles, WEIGHED AND FOUND WANTING: PUTTING THE TORONTO BLESSING INTO CONTEXT, 1995.
    Also: Articles in editions of MAINSTREAM and PROPHESY TODAY. Various audio tapes available from Banner Ministries.

13. Letter from Board of Vineyard churches to all Vineyard pastors, Dec 1995.
14. See John Goodwin, TESTING THE FRUIT OF THE VINEYARD, 1990, pp8-15.
    See also Michael Horton, ed., 'Power Evangelism' in POWER RELIGION: THE SELLING OUT OF THE EVANGELICAL CHURCH? 1992, pp61-138.
15. See Wallace Boulton, ed., THE IMPACT OF TORONTO, 1995, p19. Also David Noakes, DEALING WITH POISON IN THE POT, audio tape, CFCM 95/04, side 1. And Johannes Facius, 'Laugh? I Nearly Cried' in PROPHESY TODAY, May/June 1995, p25.
16. See Jesse Penn-Lewis, WAR ON THE SAINTS, 1912, pp47-55. And Clifford Hill, 'The Toronto Blessing: True or False?' in PROPHESY TODAY, Sept/Oct 1994, pp11-12.
17. See for example, Mike Taylor, 'The Holy Spirit and the Believer: A Look at the Scriptures' in MAINSTREAM, Spring 1995, pp6,9.
18. See for example, Robert M. Bowman, ORTHODOXY AND HERESY: A BIBLICAL GUIDE TO DOCTRINAL DISCERNMENT, 1993. And J.C. Ryle, WARNINGS TO THE CHURCHES, 1877.
19. During the Leadership Consultation on the current situation in the Charismatic churches, held in January and March 1995, by the Centre for Contemporary Ministry, the following remarks were made concerning the "catch-it-and-pass- it-on" nature of the Toronto Blessing: "David, you said that William Branham laid hands on people and that was how they received the Spirit, and then they could go and lay hands on people and they would receive the Spirit, and that was how it was passed on. This raises the concept of 'infection' and the terms being used in connection with the Toronto Blessing. In the article in the Daily Telegraph, John Arnott was quoted as saying: 'What we are seeing here is a virus from God. A wonderful, wonderful virus from God'. Now, that jarred with me and I went to the dictionary and looked up 'virus' and found four column inches of definition. 'Virus' goes back to Latin, Greek and Swahili roots, and there are two meanings of the word 'virus'. All the meanings, and their derivatives, are placed under these two meanings: One is 'poison', the other is 'venom', and all those meanings, every single one of them, is based on those two meanings. There is no other meaning of 'virus', or its derivative. But you know why people are going to Toronto? They are going to catch this thing. That is the term used; so that they can spread it to other people. It's this concept of infection." [David Forbes, THE INFLUENCE OF LATTER-RAIN TEACHING ON THE CHARISMATIC MOVEMENT, audio tape, CFCM 95/03, side 2, comments made during discussion group at end of talk].
    In contrast, Nicky Gumbel has said: "I have not had the opportunity of meeting any of the people who are supposed to be the roots [of the TB]. We are praying not for the spirit of 'X' to fill people, but for the Holy Spirit to fill them. I think it is irrelevant that so-and-so is linked with so-and-so, who once met so-and-so, who was into something that wasn't very good." [Wallace Boulton, ed., THE IMPACT OF TORONTO, 1995, p83].
    The prophet Haggai, however, would seem to warn against this view: *On the twenty-fourth day of the ninth month, in the second year of Darius, the word of the Lord came to the prophet Haggai: 'This is what the Lord Almighty says: "Ask the priests what the law says: If a person carries consecrated meat in the fold of his garment, and that fold touches some bread or stew, some wine, oil or other food, does it become consecrated?"' The priests answered, 'No.' Then Haggai said, 'If a person defiled by contact with a dead body touches one of these things, does it become defiled?' 'Yes,' the priests replied, 'it becomes defiled.' Then Haggai said, '"So it is with this people and this nation in my sight," declares the Lord. "Whatever they do and whatever they offer there is defiled."'* (Haggai 2:10-14).
20. See Tricia Tillin, BANNER HEADLINES NEWS UPDATE, BMX22, Dec 1995.
21. See, for example, Stanley Jebb, REFORMATION, RENEWAL, ROMANISM, audio tape. (A

warning to Evangelicals/Charismatics against Ecumenism).

Also J.C. Ryle, WARNINGS TO THE CHURCHES, 1877. M. De Semlyen, ALL ROADS LEAD TO ROME:THE ECUMENICAL MOVEMENT, 1993.

Dave Hunt, 'Evangelicals and Catholics, Declaration of Unity: The Gospel Betrayed' in THE BEREAN CALL, May 1994, quoted in MAINSTREAM, Summer 1994, pp10,11.

Dave Hunt, A WOMAN RIDES THE BEAST: THE ROMAN CATHOLIC CHURCH IN THE LAST DAYS, 1994, chapters 22-28. Various audio tapes available from Banner Ministries. Also the March/April 1996 edition of DISCERNMENT (P.O. box 129, Lapeer, USA), which focuses on Ecumenism/Church unity.

22.See Tricia Tillin, 'Thy Word is Truth' in MAINSTREAM, Winter 1993, p9. Also Robert M. Bowman, ORTHODOXY AND HERESY: A BIBLICAL GUIDE TO DOCTRINAL DISCERNMENT, 1993, pp27-32.

23.See David Pawson, WHEN JESUS RETURNS, 1995, p72. Dave Hunt, BEYOND SEDUCTION: THE RETURN TO BIBLICAL CHRISTIANITY, 1987, pp3-4. J.C. Ryle, WARNINGS TO THE CHURCHES, 1877, pp103-107;110-112;127-128.

24.See Tricia Tillin, 'Birth of the Manchild' in MAINSTREAM, Spring 1995, pp1-5 for the eschatology being taught at some Vineyard churches, referred to by John Wimber in his letter to Vineyard pastors, Dec 1995, under the heading 'Other Concerns'.

25.See for example, Stuart Dool, A TABLE IN THE WILDERNESS, audio tape, Dec 1995. Also Yacov Prasch, THE TORONTO BLESSING IS IT? UNDERSTANDING OF THE GOLDEN CALF, video tape, Moriel Ministries, 1995.

APPENDIX 1

There is no doubt that the Alpha Course (which originated at Holy Trinity, Brompton, London) is the fastest-growing and largest-selling course in Christian basics available today. What are we to make of it?

The large number of churches right across denominational barriers using the course has been seen as one of the great evangelistic successes of recent years. It is claimed to be the simplest and most effective means of telling others about Jesus Christ!

Clear structure

The key to its success almost certainly lies in the structure of the course. There are ten meetings including such topics as: 'Who is Jesus?', 'Why did Jesus die?', 'Why and how should I read the Bible?', 'Why and how do I pray?', 'How can I resist evil?' 'What about the church?' Groups are encouraged to structure each meeting to begin with a meal and include time for discussion. While many of the topics are standard material for basics courses, the idea of building relationships through a meal together, is perhaps a key to what makes Alpha different. In addition to the weekly meetings, there is an Alpha weekend (or Saturday) which allows greater opportunity for fellowship and ministry as well as talks.

Churches are free to use or adapt the talk outlines produced by Nicky Gumbel, or to play the audio/video tapes of Nicky delivering the talks at Holy Trinity, Brompton. The course material is available in book form as *Questions of Life* by Nicky Gumbel, and there are a number of supporting books and videos which provide back-up for churches using the material. The talks are well written, Bible-based and use many familiar illustrations and arguments.

Problems

However, I do have some problems with the course. One of the clearly-stated principles of the course is that: 'Evangelism is integrally related to the supernatural display of the power of the Holy Spirit.' The explanation of this makes it clear that it does *not* refer to the work of the Holy Spirit in convicting of sin and in regeneration, but rather to the expectation of visible and audible manifestations of the Spirit at work primarily in healing and speaking in tongues.

Indeed the *Training Manual* describes 'a model for ministry' which includes the following instructions: 'Encourage the person to start to speak in another language – tell him/her you will do so yourself.' This seems to be in accord with the teaching given in the talk 'How can I be filled with the Spirit?' which concentrates on the gift of tongues and includes practical instructions on how to pray for that particular gift.

Similarly, one whole talk is devoted to 'Does God heal today?' and includes practical instruction on how to pray for healing. The emphasis on technique rather than faith in these areas seems to me to be less than helpful, and fails to address these issues in their true biblical context. But I have reservations about the assumption that it is always God's will to make such supernatural displays of the power of the Holy Spirit in the context of evangelism. There was at least one occasion when Jesus actually refused to perform miracles because the crowds were more interested in the spectacle than in his message. We are not immune from the same problem.

Lifestyle and doctrine?

My *second* problem has to do with the general content of the course. Scripture tells us that salvation comes through hearing the gospel, and I would expect any course aimed at non-christians to concentrate primarily on the facts of the gospel. The Alpha Course deals with the basics of the gospel in two sessions: 'Who is Jesus?' and 'Why did Jesus die?' While these are unequivocal gospel presentations, the remainder of the course deals essentially with what might be described as Christian living.

One of the problems of proclaiming in the gospel in a post-modern world is that the culture itself warms much more readily to lifestyle than to doctrine. But the Christian lifestyle is not Christian faith.

When we used an adapted version of the course in our church, non-christians were left behind by about the sixth week. They still had very fundamental questions about what Christians believe which were not answered by talking about how Christians live, and for this reason the course seemed more suited to people who have already made a commitment to Christ. I am sure that many people are being converted through the Alpha course, but I have a suspicion that some of those people are being converted to a Christian lifestyle rather than to Christ.

Commendation

For all these reservations there is much to commend in the Alpha course. In an adapted form, we have found it an excellent nurture course for new Christians and a challenging refresher course for more mature Christians. The meal together each week cements friendships and the Saturday away allows the opportunity to discuss spiritual matters in a more relaxed and informal setting. We have found our church members enthusiastic enough about the course to attend a second time with others they have invited, which must be good news!

And the Alpha course is certainly addressing two significant needs. There are many people who are willing to attend a course like Alpha to hear what Christianity has to offer. Our society is searching for answers to spiritual questions. Whether we use Alpha or something else, our fellowships must take this willingness seriously.

But the success of the Alpha material also shows that our churches are crying out for proven resources. Whether this simply reflects a loss of confidence by churches and individuals in their own ability to proclaim the gospel effectively is unclear. But if the Alpha Course is encouraging Christians in evangelism, then it deserves some credit for that at least.

Ian Lewis, St Bartholemew's, Bath.
Reproduced from Evangelicals Now *December 1995 with permission.*

APPENDIX 2

The gospel of love.... or the gospel of God?

The book of Acts is the only biblical account of how the apostles preached the gospel. This is important because it is often assumed that the four Gospels and the Epistles are also direct sources of how the gospel message should be preached.

The gospels were written for churches or for people who were already believers, or who had recently believed. They gave information about 'all that Jesus began to do and to teach...' As is generally agreed the gospel of John is to some extent different in that it was written 'that you may believe and have life in His name', however the second part of the book (from chapters 13 onwards) are intended for the intimate disciples of Jesus.

The Epistles and Revelation were, of course, all written to believers or churches. Thus they were not intended as gospel messages.

So only Acts can give any idea of the *content* of gospel messages preached to unbelievers – both Jew and Gentile.

The sermons contained in the book are found in the following chapters : Acts 2:14-40 (J), 3:12-26 (J). 7:2-53 (J)*. 10:34-43 (G), 13:16-41 (J), 14:15-17 (G), 17:22-31, (G) 22:2-21* (J), 24:10-21*, 26:2-29*.
(J) proclamation before predominantly Jewish audience, and (G) represents proclamation before a predominantly Gentile audience.Those marked with a *represent legal defences before a court.

Briefly, what are the main themes?
1. That Jesus is Messiah, fulfilling the Law and the prophets. That he was crucified and rose from the dead and that through repentance there is forgiveness and the gift of the Holy Spirit.
2. In addition, for Gentiles: that God is Creator and Judge who now calls all to repent by faith in Jesus.

What is conspicuous by its absence is any mention of the Love of God is these sermons. In fact the word love does not occur in Acts!

This is almost a complete reversal of current trends in gospel preaching. These days 'God loves you' is more or less where people start! Here sadly is the bad news; that is not the gospel! Sinners are under Wrath. Yes, they *are* loved by God, yet unless they repent and turn to Christ, they remain under Wrath – they will not *know* that God loves them, indeed they cannot know. Therefore telling them that 'God loves them anyway' will lead either to pride (I am worth something!) or dismissal, 'who cares!' Frankly, the last thing middle-class Westerners need to hear is that God loves them! Rather the reverse is true; that God demands their repentance, for then and only then can they discover that God really does love them.

Even in the gospels Jesus does not *tell* sinners that He loves them (He befriended them, but that is action, not a matter of words). One interesting example of this point is found in Mark 10:17ff; the story of the rich young ruler. In v21 *the readers* are specifically told that Jesus loved him. But Jesus never tells *him* that! When the man goes away sorrowfully, Jesus does not shout out after him, "I love you!"

It is intriguing to note that all other references to love in the gospels are not part of proclamation (look them up in the concordance). Even in the gospel of John, references to the love of God occur very rarely in the record of Jesus' public ministry: and the majority of these are from chapter 13 onward, when Jesus is with the twelve disciples.

Earlier references are: John 3:16 (which is either John's commentary or part of a one-to-one conversation of Jesus with Nicodemus, and not therefore public proclamation). John 5:42, John 11:5, 13, 36, John 12:43. None of these references are directly connected to the message proclaimed.

What then of the stories of the Prodigal son and the Lost sheep? Both have been used as gospel parables, and in a sense they are. However, the context – particularly in the case of the prodigal son – is often not recognised. He is, after all a prodigal *son*. In other words, he has a Father before he leaves! This is not true of a Gentile sinner (such as most of us are). We do not start off with God as our Father, wander away and then get welcomed back! Jesus' ministry was primarily to the *children, the lost sheep of the house of Israel* (Matt 15:24 and Mark 6:27, compare also Galatians 2:15). These stories were addressed to Jewish people and were about coming *back* to God as their Father. We *can* use them as part of the gospel message but they are not the main message for Gentiles who are not children of God except by adoption through the Cross of Christ.

I have very serious concerns that we evangelicals/charismatics are preaching another gospel, 'the gospel of love' rather than the gospel of 'repent and believe' – which is the gospel of God.

Philip Foster
St Matthew's Church, Cambridge